Selling Out

John Goodwin

Published in association with
The Basic Skills Agency

Hodder & Stoughton
A MEMBER OF THE HODDER HEADLINE GROUP

Acknowledgements
Cover: Stuart Williams
Illustrations: Doug Gray

Orders: please contact Bookpoint Ltd, 130 Milton Park, Abingdon, Oxon OX14 4SB. Telephone: (44) 01235 827720, Fax: (44) 01235 400454. Lines are open from 9.00–6.00, Monday to Saturday, with a 24 hour message answering service. Email address: orders@bookpoint.co.uk

British Library Cataloguing in Publication Data
A catalogue record for this title is available from The British Library

ISBN 0 340 80081 X

First published 2001
Impression number 10 9 8 7 6 5 4 3 2
Year   2007 2006 2005 2004 2003 2002 2001

Typeset by SX Composing DTP, Rayleigh, Essex.
Printed in Great Britain for Hodder & Stoughton Educational, a division of Hodder Headline Plc, 338 Euston Road, London NW1 3BH by Athenaeum Press, Gateshead, Tyne and Wear.

About the play

The People

- **Ravi**, a young football player
- **Joe**, a young football player
- **Danny**, a young football player
- **Benny**, the coach
- **The Football Crowd**
- **The Referee**

The Place

Sutton United Youth Football Club

What's Happening

Ravi, **Joe** and **Danny** *are playing a football match.*
Benny *looks on from the touch line.*

Act 1

Scene 1

Crowd	UNITED!
	UNITED!
Joe	Pass it.
Ravi	Pass the ball.
Benny	Pass the ball, Danny.
	Pass it to Ravi.
Joe	Yeah.
Benny	Well done, Danny.
Joe	Great pass, Danny.
Benny	Now go for it, Ravi.
Danny	Go for goal.
Crowd	GIVE US A GOAL!
	GIVE US A GOAL!
Joe	Man on Ravi.
Benny	Look out, Ravi.
Danny	Man on Ravi!

1

The Referee blows a whistle for a foul on Ravi.

Benny	Foul!
Joe	You dirty fouler.
Crowd	SEND HIM OFF.
	SEND HIM OFF.
Benny	Don't move, Ravi.
	I'll be with you.
Ravi	I think I've broken my leg.
Benny	Easy now.
Ravi	The pain's terrible.
Referee	We'll need a stretcher.
	I'll blow my whistle for half time.
	The Referee blows the whistle.

Scene 2

Half time on the pitch.
Ravi has been taken to hospital.

Danny Do you think he'll be OK, Benny?
Benny Yes.
Joe Do you reckon his leg is broken?
Benny We've got to forget about Ravi.
Danny We can't forget about him.
Benny We have to.
　　　　Think about the game.
　　　　We're one–nil ahead.
　　　　Danny, play in defence.
Danny Right.
Benny All of you, play hard.
　　　　Don't let in any soft goals, Joe.
　　　　Keep your eye on the ball.
Joe Right.
Benny We can still win this one.

The Referee's whistle goes for the start
of the second half.

Crowd UNITED.
UNITED.
IF YOU ALL LIKE UNITED
CLAP YOUR HANDS.
IF YOU ALL LIKE UNITED
CLAP YOUR HANDS.
IF YOU ALL LIKE UNITED
IF YOU ALL LIKE UNITED
IF YOU ALL LIKE UNITED
CLAP YOUR HANDS.

Benny Come on United.
Watch their number nine.

Joe Look out, defence.

Benny Look out, Joe.

Joe Tackle him, Danny.

Benny He's through our defence.

Joe Tackle him.

Benny He's going for goal.

Joe He's in the penalty area.

Benny Tackle him, Danny.

Joe Tackle him, Danny.

Benny   Not like that!

The Referee's whistle blows for a foul.

Referee   That was a foul.
              A dirty foul.
Benny   Come off it, Ref.
Referee   Yellow card.
Danny   What?
Referee   Penalty.
Benny   Not a penalty, Ref.

The Referee's whistle blows for the penalty.

Referee   Penalty to Rovers.
Danny   It's all my fault.
Benny   You've got to save it, Joe.
Joe   Which way will he shoot?
Danny   Come on, Joe.

Crowd	COME ON JOE
	COME ON JOE
Joe	He's going to shoot to the right.
Danny	He's scored . . .
	No he hasn't.
	Joe's . . .
Benny	Saved it.
Crowd	WHAT A SAVE
	WHAT A SAVE
Benny	Great save, Joe.
Danny	Well done, Joe.
Benny	You've saved the game.
Crowd	UNITED
	UNITED
	WHAT A WIN
	WHAT A WIN

The Referee's whistle goes for the end of the match. Everybody cheers.

Act 2

In Benny's office. Six weeks later.
Ravi *comes into the office on crutches.*

Benny   How goes it, Ravi?
Ravi   Terrible.
Benny   Why's that?
Ravi   It hurts worse than when I did it.
Benny   You should take it easy.
Ravi   I can't take it easy.
    I can't sleep at nights.
    For six long weeks it's been like this.
Benny   That's bad news.
Ravi   Yes.
Benny   The team miss you.
Ravi   I miss football.
Benny   So when is it going to get better?
Ravi   I don't know.
    Sometimes it seems like
    I'll never play again.

Benny	You're too good a player to miss so many games.
Ravi	I just wish it would get better.
Benny	How much do you wish?
Ravi	What?
Benny	I said, how much do you wish your leg was better?
Ravi	You know how much.
Benny	Yes I do. I might have something to help you.
Ravi	What?
Benny	Something from Benny's top drawer.

Benny *opens the top drawer of his desk
and takes out a small packet. He gives it
to* **Ravi**.

	A few of these should sort you out.
Ravi	What are they?
Benny	Don't ask questions, Ravi.
Ravi	Just tell me what they are.
Benny	A little something to build up your muscles.
Ravi	Oh yeah?

Benny	To help build up your muscles so you can get back in the game soon. Take a few of those and you could be playing in a few weeks. Just think of that, Ravi.
Ravi	They're drugs, aren't they? I don't want any drugs.
Benny	They're harmless.
Ravi	No they're not. I know what these are . . . they are steroid drugs. Athletes take these, then get banned for life.
Benny	They're nothing like that. Do you want to play again this season, Ravi?
Ravi	Of course I want to play again this season. I can do it without drugs.
Benny	Are you sure of that?
Ravi	Yes.

Act 3

At Ravi's house. A few weeks later.

Danny So we won three–nil.
Ravi Oh.
Danny Elroy's taken your
position as striker.
He had a great match.
He scored two brilliant goals.
Ravi Oh.
Danny How's your leg?
Ravi Not much better.
Danny You should come up
and see us play.
We're going to win
the league this year.
Ravi Really?
Danny So are you going to
come and see the next match?
Ravi I'll see.

Act 4

In Benny's office.

Joe   You wanted to see me.
Benny Yes. Take a seat, Joe.
Joe   OK.
Benny You've been playing goalie
          really well the last few months.
Joe   The whole team have been
          playing like a dream.
Benny Yes.
Joe   Ten goals in three matches
          can't be bad.
Benny But you've made some
          blinding saves, Joe.
          None better than saving that
          penalty.
          That was brilliant.
Joe   Bit of luck.
Benny More than luck, Joe.
Joe   Not really.

Benny	We are six points clear
	at the top of the league.
Joe	With a game in hand.
Benny	So we can relax a bit.
Joe	You can never relax in football.

Benny *opens his top drawer and pulls out an envelope.*

Benny	Something for you, Joe.
Joe	For me?
Benny	A present for being a
	brilliant goalie.
	Open it.

Joe *opens the envelope.*

Joe	A load of cash.
Benny	A hundred quid to be exact.
Joe	A hundred quid!
Benny	You've got real talent.
	Talent to go to the very top.
Joe	I can't take this.
Benny	You'll get to the top
	and learn to take presents.
Joe	What do you mean?
Benny	Take the cash and maybe . . .

Joe	Maybe what?
Benny	Maybe relax a bit the next game.
	It wouldn't matter if you let
	in a couple of goals.
	Just for the next match.
Joe	You want me to let in goals.
Benny	Got it in one.
Joe	Why?
Benny	I need us to lose the match.
Joe	What for?
Benny	There's money in this. Big money.
Joe	You want me to fix the match.
	Well I'm not going to.
	No way. Keep your cash.
Benny	Don't be in such a rush.
	Think about it.
	You could use a hundred quid,
	couldn't you?
	And that's just for starters.
	There'll be more in the future.
Joe	You don't bribe me.
Benny	Steady, Joe.
	I can easily find another goalie.
	Just think about it.

Act 5

Scene 1

At Ravi's house.

Ravi   He offered me drugs.
Joe   He didn't.
Ravi   He did.
Joe   You didn't take them?
Ravi   No.
       But I was tempted.
       Hobbling about on crutches
       week after week isn't much fun.
       I was thinking about giving them
       a try.
Joe   He offered me cash.
Ravi   What for?
Joe   For fixing a game.
Ravi   You didn't take it.

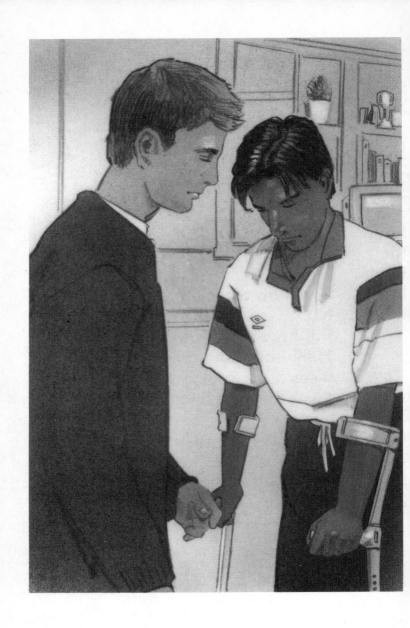

Joe	No. But just think what you could buy with a hundred quid. And there'd be a load more dosh to follow. All I had to do was say yes.
Ravi	One simple little word.
Joe	We've got to stop him.
Ravi	How?
Joe	Shop him.
Ravi	How are we going to do that then?
Joe	I know exactly how we'll do it. You and I are going to pay Benny a visit in his office.

Scene 2

In Benny's office.

Joe   So we've been thinking it over.

Benny   Sounds good to me, boys.

Ravi   Yeah, I reckon those steroids
will do the trick.
I mean, you did want me to take
them Benny, didn't you?

Benny   Of course I did, Ravi.

Ravi   Even though they are illegal.

Benny   Ravi . . . everybody needs to bend
the rules now and again don't they?
That's all we are doing.

Joe   I could really use a hundred quid
right now, Benny.

Benny   Of course you could.

Joe   Just to let in a goal or two.
I mean, every goalie has an off day
now and then.

Benny   Of course they do.

Joe	So you're going to pay me a hundred quid to lose a few games for you? So you can do a dodgy deal and win a few bets. Have I got it right, Benny?
Benny	You got it in one. I can let you have the money right now.
Ravi	Drugs and bribes.
Benny	That's putting it a bit strong, Ravi.
Ravi	Is it?
Benny	This is just to help you two lads out.
Joe	Really?
Ravi	Make me a junkie . . . that's helping me out, is it?
Joe	And make me take a bribe to lose a game. What kind of sportsman would do that?

Benny	What's going on?
Ravi	We're going to shop you, Benny.
Joe	Let everybody know the truth about you.
Benny	Oh really?
Ravi	Yes.
Joe	Yes.
Benny	You've got no proof. Nobody will believe two kids.

Joe	But we have got proof.
	Show him the recorder, Ravi.

Ravi *takes a small tape recorder out of his pocket.*

Ravi	It's all here. Listen.

Ravi *rewinds the tape and plays back the conversation.*

Joe	We've got you taped, Benny.
	Clear evidence.
Benny	Nobody is going to believe you.
	You're just two kids.
Joe	Eleven kids actually, Benny.
Ravi	Yes.

Joe	Eleven kids and one tape recorder.
	All the evidence we need
	to prove that
	you offered drugs.
Ravi	Or tried to bribe us.
Joe	There's no way out.
Ravi	No place to hide.
Joe	No place in football for you.
Ravi	You're finished, Benny.
Crowd	UNITED
	UNITED

The whistle goes for the end of the match.

If you have enjoyed reading this book, you may be interested in other titles in the *Livewire* series.

The Library
Romeo, Romeo
Doing Macbeth
Night Fishing
Place Your Bets

The Mimic
Football Clones
The Day Trippers
The Chosen One